MUSINGS WITH THE
ANGEL OF DEATH

Praise for MUSINGS WITH THE ANGEL OF DEATH

"Through decades of research, Simcha Paull Raphael brought us close to distant, ancient and esoteric Jewish texts that illumine our understanding of Jewish views of death and the afterlife. With this collection of poetry, he now invites us to sit by his side at a café, sipping a cup of tea or coffee, to reflect together on some of the most tender, precious and challenging moments of life. It is a sumptuous repast!"

Barbara E. Breitman, D. Min.
Director of Jewish Spiritual Direction Training
Reconstructionist Rabbinical College
Wyncote, PA

"In this wry and wistful volume of poems Simcha Paull Raphael shares his existential musings on the mysteries and limitations of these mortal lives we live. Raphael's vulnerable, moving, often comical outpourings of the heart make us love him, love ourselves, and laugh knowingly at the human condition we share."

Rabbi Tirzah Firestone, Ph.D.
Author of *The Receiving: Reclaiming Jewish Women's Wisdom,* and *Wounds into Wisdom: Healing Intergenerational Jewish Trauma*

"From sitting shiva to sitting in Starbucks, from the challenge of birth to facing mortality, Simcha Paull Raphael reaches deep into his own heart to connect with our hearts through his poetry. *Musings with the Angel of Death* is a meaningful collection taking readers from heights to depths."

Rabbi Elyse Goldstein,
City Shul, Toronto, ON
Author of *ReVisions: Seeing Torah Through a Feminist Lens*

"*Musings with the Angel of Death* is an open-hearted, richly-textured collection of poetry, a grounded meditation on life, love, and loss. Simcha Paull Raphael takes his readers on a journey of discovery that reveals that the ordinary is the very thing that makes life exquisite, and extraordinary. Readers—sit by the fire, enjoy a poem, and discover that you are not walking the path of life alone."

Cole Imperi
Founder, School of American Thanatology

"Simcha Paull Raphael's poetic voice is personal, intimate, courageous, and inviting. Each poem is a doorway inside the thirty-six room mansion of his soul as he gently takes us on a tour of his own inner life. The poems have the feel of a good friend inviting the reader to meet his family members, and inspiring us to reflect upon our own. Each poem lights up a unique mirror neuron so that we end up seeing ourselves, our families, our lives, our deaths through his. His conversational voice about death transforms fear into the desire to live life even more fully at every moment. Like a good collection of memorabilia, this anthology is one to save and savor."

Rabbi David Zaslow
Havurah Shir Hadash, Ashland, OR
Author of *Reimagining Exodus: A Story of Freedom*

"In *Musings with the Angel of Death* Simcha Paull Raphael gives voice to the deep and expansive layers of meeting and embracing the "valley of shadows" without fear. Exploring and encountering the fragility of life in the face of loss and mortality, he provides us with a gateway to the world most of us resist until the end. Raphael's poetry of love, life, and longing touch the heart and soul reminding us how we might live more fully with these angels of mortality in a way that makes life more precious. Take this journey and be enlivened by it!"

Rabbi Shawn Zevit
Mishkan Shalom, Philadelphia, PA
Author of *Offerings of the Heart: Money and Values in Faith Community*, and co-editor of *Brother Keepers: New Perspectives on Jewish Masculinity*

"The old shall be renewed,
and the new shall be made holy."
— Rabbi Avraham Yitzhak Kook

Albion-Andalus Books
P. O. Box 19852
Boulder, CO 80308
albionandalus.com

Design by Albion-Andalus Books

Cover design by Scott Fray

ISBN-13 (PB): 978-1-953220-37-0

ISBN-13 (HC): 978-1-953220-38-7

MUSINGS WITH THE ANGEL OF DEATH

POEMS OF LOVE, LIFE, AND LONGING

Simcha Paull Raphael

Albion
Andalus

Boulder, Colorado
2024

Dedicated to my parents,
Harold Paull (1917-2002) &
Rose Paull (1923-2011),
who encouraged my creativity
and allowed me to become myself

Contents

Wisdom Years

Love and Death, Mourning and Meaning

MIDLIFE, PARENTING AND MARRIAGE

CREATIVITY AND IMAGINATION

JUVENILIA

FOREWORD

Since the early 1990's, Dr. Simcha Paull Raphael
has been teaching and writing about grief, loss,
memory, and hope. As a teacher of Jewish views of
the afterlife, he has delved into Jewish writings of a
variety of eras about the soul, reincarnation, and
rituals related to death. He has made Jewish texts
about death and dying accessible to contemporary
Jews, and has offered classes and workshops around
the country that make Jewish death literature a
respected topic. In particular, Raphael has invited
people to consider their own mortality. He has
encouraged us to have conversations about death, to
acknowledge our grief regarding our own finite lives
and those of others we cherish. He has invited us to
make sure that when we talk about being human,
death has a seat at the table.

By doing this work, Raphael has made it easier
for us to talk about loss. In an era when death
was something many Jews avoided talking about,
Raphael reminded us of traditional Jewish language
for dealing with what we all know is real: change, the
impermanence of physical existence, and the power
of love despite these inevitable transformations. And
Raphael has reminded us of Jewish conceptions of
the soul. By focusing not only on the fact of death but

on how Judaism has sought to transcend it, Raphael has given us hope, despite our fear of the unknown.

It is important to note that matters like death, love, and loss are never entirely abstract. While it is true that these things are part of the universal human condition, each of us experiences them differently. What matters more than the unavoidability of our life's limits as a philosophical concept, is the particular love and longing that we bear toward our families, our beloveds, and our world. It is that particular love that drives us to understand our finitude, and that drives civilizations to create myths, legends, rituals, and ideas that address death and mortality.

In this volume of poems, Simcha Paull Raphael has done the brave work of exposing his own emotional life, the inner workings of his drive to address mortality and immortality. In a sense, he has let us know the behind-the-scenes of his academic and spiritual work. The poems in this volume deal with Raphael's own experience of mortality—as he writes, "the never-ending drumbeat of time." In his first poem, Raphael admits that many years of talking to others about death hasn't quite reconciled him to his own. Like Moses, he pleads with the angel of death to spare him, but she is not impressed; as we all know, she never is.

Beneath the wings of this angel, Raphael writes about "the ghosts of grief": his father, his mother, and the world itself in the shadow of climate catastrophe. He details his experience of saying kaddish, the feeling of being an orphan, and the complexities of mourning for a man who never cried. Raphael writes about Jewish mourning from burial and shiva to unveiling and *yizkor*, and the restless grief these rituals cannot quite cure.

Raphael also addresses other parts of the lifecycle: the experience of being an adoptive father, of celebrating a son's bar mitzvah, of lauding a seven-year-old tomboy. Yet he often returns to the loss found even in moments of joy, the "end of boyhood" that is part of coming of age, the small disillusionments of marriage, the "he said, she said" of domestic conflicts, the sand castles that don't last forever, and in the end the knowing that we must "be grateful nothing more was destroyed." Raphael also writes about his own creative process, again while acknowledging ways that an artist's acts of creation valiantly try to beat back existential questions about existence, but cannot quite manage it.

Raphael allows himself, even as he feels like an observer, to acknowledge that "I too am part of this/ eternal melding, meeting/of earth and atmosphere, land and sky." Raphael identifies, despite the vicissitudes and daily grumbles of life, as "a single, solitary soul/interwoven into the woof and warp/ of the very fabric of creation itself." By sharing, through these poems, the undercurrents of mortality and immortality in his own life, Raphael does the same work he has always done, which is to remind us both of our ephemerality and of our eternity. When we read the fascinating myths he has collected in his scholarly work, we can now understand what drove him to collect them.

Musings with the Angel of Death: Poems of Love, Life, and Longing is a journey exploring the mystery of death, love and loss, a journey which we all must embark upon sooner or later.

Rabbi Jill Hammer, Ph.D.
Director of Spiritual Education
Academy for Jewish Religion, Yonkers, NY

PREFACE

I have been composing poetry, on and off, for over fifty years. Poetry is radically different both in style and content from my other writings, publications which are more scholarly and academic. This selection of thirty-six poems represents a cross-section of what I have written over the years. Though not quite a memoir of my life in poetry, this book is at least a glimpse of the journey I have traveled.

Above all, I offer a heartfelt tribute of gratitude and appreciation to my wife, Rabbi Geela Rayzel Raphael, who has been a beloved friend and co-parenting partner on my life journey for almost forty years. She more than anyone else has witnessed and participated with me in the oys and joys of raising a family, and in the trials and tribulations of dealing with our own parents aging and dying. During the past thirty-plus years we raised and launched our two children, who are each fashioning their own pathways of creative artistry in the world. In spite of the vicissitudes and challenges of marriage and parenting—as evidenced in poems herein—we have survived and thrived, and are aging gracefully as lifelong companions and friends. I look forward to more years together.

Additionally, I am grateful for the opportunity I had to participate in Mystery School workshops with Dr. Jean Houston, for four years—from 1997-2000. Jean is truly a wizard at catalyzing the creativity muses for her students, and I acknowledge the influence of her creative teaching style in awakening and re-vitalizing my own process of writing poetry.

This is the seventh book in the *Jewish Life, Death and Transition* series, published by Albion-Andalus Books, in collaboration with the Da'at Institute for Death Awareness, Advocacy and Training. I thank Netanel Miles-Yépez of Albion-Andalus Books for his vision to create this series, and Daniel Jami for his thoughtful and gentle editorial wisdom midwifing this book to publication. Additionally, I want to add a tribute of appreciation to my friend Scott Fray for his awesome artistic acumen and creativity in designing the cover for this book.

And finally, at this stage in my life journey I am filled with gratitude for the opportunity to share the fruits of my creativity with others. In devotion, I acknowledge the Source of Life, the Holy One of Blessing, who has given us life and vitality, sustained us and brought us to this moment.

Simcha Paull Raphael
Melrose Park, PA
October 22nd, 2023
(my parents' wedding anniversary)

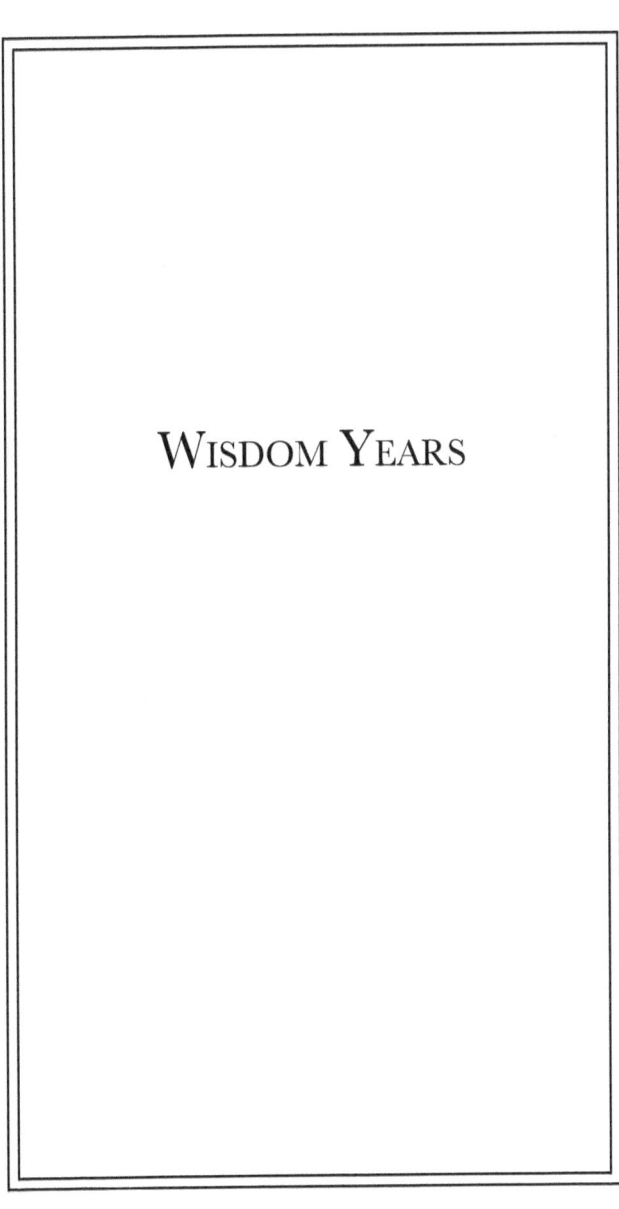

WISDOM YEARS

THE ANGEL OF DEATH AWAITS

Off in the distance
At the edge of the horizon of my life
I sense the Angel of Death
Patiently, dispassionately
Waiting for me
With unambiguous certainty
That we shall rendezvous
Someday.

I recognize her
Loving, radiant and luminescent
She is a she, or maybe a they
Sitting in silence at the boundary line between
The finite and the infinite
Between here and eternity
Between this that I know
And I know not what.

Peering deeply towards the edge of time
I see her luminosity, recognize her wisdom
I am curious
But uncertain how to respond
I want to shout out: "I am not afraid of you!"
But to be truthful
Fearless in the face of death I am not
And besides, I am sure she would
See through the lie.

Yet I feel we know each other very well
Or not at all
It is a peculiar dance we've done together
For so, so long
She is a powerful and mystifying shape shifter
Once upon a time
A Grim Reaper that tormented my youth
I used to see her, or was it him, or perhaps they
As a tyrannical wrathful expediter of fate
Cruel, heartless fate
Precise, swift and harsh.

But over the years
We have made peace
At least a detente
The cascading rhythms of time
Have yielded mutual respect
Even as she watches over my shoulder
I keep my distance
Following the echoes of inner callings
Creatively keeping busy and distracted
Doing stuff, consuming stuff, eating stuff
Facebook stuff, email stuff, Amazon stuff
Mindless numbing stuff
I've become a master of all kinds of
Efficacious and totally ineffective ways of
Pretending the Angel of Death
Is not just around the corner at all times.

But tonight
Something deep inside is stirring
Piercing my somnambulant, smug complacency
The cycles of the season
The never-ending drumbeat of time
And another year around the sun
Are all coalescing in this moment
Beckoning me to peer towards
The edge of the abyss
Where she, he, they, adversary and ally all in one
Awaits patiently, dispassionately.

Am I really ready for an encounter
With that enigmatic being of light?
Holding my breath, I look up
She smiles and telegraphs to my mind
"I'm here waiting.
Any day is a good day for being born
Any day is a good day for dying."

Holy shit! I am not ready for this.
I have read lots of books
I have even written a few
And talked to oh so many people
About the Angel of Death
I've spent hours and hours
Holding the hands of traumatized bereaved
But I am not sure I am ready

For this Angel of Death lady
Even if I can see her pulsating heart radiating love
I'm just not sure.

Can't I just check my Facebook status first
There must be something I can do besides…

"No" she says, "I am here, I am not going away
Your life depends on it."
With piercing penetration to the core of my being
Seeing into the destiny of my soul over lifetimes
She implants in my mind one word, nothing more
One word, "Prepare!"

And in an instantaneous visionary flash
I see a panoramic vision of my entire life
From birth to death
(Though the death part is mostly fuzzy,
Not yet in focus).

I see the nun who saved me from death at birth
Giving me the breath of life
I feel the fears and tears
Of the love and lies in my family of origin story
I feel the loneliness of the smart boy-child
The insecure arrogance of the well-dressed teen
I see the abuse traumas
Etched into my being for a lifetime
I see the sadness of death, too many, too often
I see the glorious days of gifts and the blessings

Of opportunities for learning the life of spirit
The teachers, teachings, writings
So many unique experiences and opportunities
Bequeathed to me
I feel the the growing pains
And the ravages abuse and addiction
I see the loves, the lasciviousness of single life
Soon followed by the blessing of marriage
Children, family, home
Wonderful work opportunities
Teaching, writing expressing the love
And the passions of my life
As I moved from the fringe to the frontier
Deaths of parents and the emergence
Of the gentle years of aging
And I see lots and lots of *hamsas*
Lots and lots of *chachkas*
And so, so much more
Collections of random, relevant
Ultimately meaningless memorabilia.

I pause with great gratitude for all the blessings
And notice the Angel of Death is still there.
"What now?" I ask
"I am not ready to go
I have more work to do," I say—
She is not moved, not impressed.
Then I pour my heart out
"I have more love to bring into the world
I have more wisdom to share.

Look at my life, look at my life
My wife, my children
Look at the friendship and love
That surrounds me.
I need to grow the love, deepen the wisdom."

Suddenly, the scene changes
The Being of Light merges with all that is
Reaching towards the heavens
Reaching her arms upwards and outwards
Offering blessings

Yivarechecha Adonai viyishmirecha
Ya'er Adonai panav elecha veechuneka
Yeesa Adonai panav elecha viyasem lecha shalom

May the blessings of God rest upon you
May God's peace abide with you
May God's presence illuminate your heat
Now and forever more.

"Do what you are here to do,
Love those you are here to love,
But remember, I will be back!"
And when I looked up
She was gone
Beyond the horizon
And I know that I am blessed and
Grateful for what is

And in response to that wonderful encounter
With that Angel of Death lady
I affirm my commitment to life and love.

Today is the first day of the rest of my life.

Lo Aleicha HaMelacha Ligmor
(It is Not Your Duty
to Complete the Task)

At the center of all my sorrows
I have frequently felt a presence
That was not mine alone
I know I am not the only one
Who encounters such feelings
Repeatedly I become present
To these stealth invaders
There they are in my waking daze
In otherworldly dreams
And in all-too-many sleepless nights.
At both predictable and inopportune moments
I find myself enveloped
By waves and waves of enigmatic emotions
Leaving me possessed by a presence
That is not mine alone
Isn't that what it means to be alive?
To be human?

In the ever-flowing, ever-changing stream
Of mindless clutter and mindful chatter
I feel the presence of the
Gnawing loss of love and family
Lost brothers
Dead parents
So so many friends whose lives ended early

All those ghosts of grief are with me all the time
As I try to make my way through aging, sage-ing
The mysteries of love and marriage
And late-life parenting.
In between the personal chronicles and sagas
Of this man's life
Are the roaring, raging tragic tales
Constant stories that invade my psyche
Leaving body-mind
Overwhelmed, emotionally paralyzed
Never-ending and persistent stories
Of war and dead children
Hatred and xenophobia
One damn climate catastrophe after another
Delivered in precipitous waves
Through the complexity of internet intensity
The numbing din and clatter of
Monotonous cable tv
And miscellaneous, multi-phonic
Sometimes just plain
Soul-destroying satellite radio
Proffering a persistent panoply of news
Illuminating and highlighting the pain
Of an alluring yet ravaged
Blue planet in deep space
Burning up, wind swept, flooded
By rising coast lines
Choking on toxic poison air
No longer aromatic like it was
In the pristine Laurentian Mountain air

Of my youth.
Instead each day I discover myself
Surrounded by toxic waste, polluted skies
Way, way too much plastic and garbage
As I hear and digest
Horrific insidious tales of vanishing species
Decimated rain forests
Desiccated river beds and valleys
Toxic greedy politicians
Vengeful religious zealots
Caring not for life of the other.
I feel all this anguishing pain in my body
And I know I cannot fully purge
This crazy kaleidoscope of suffering and sorrow
Anymore than I can stop the melting glaciers
Erupting earthquakes and tsunamis
Hurricanes, tornadoes, floods
And so many other unpredictable
Unavoidable fatalities
And outbreaks of hell on earth.

And in the face of all of this
I wake up each morning
Shower and shave
Brush my teeth and clothe myself for the day
And somehow find me—whatever that might be
In the maze and morass of planetary angst.
Vigilantly I remember to stop
Quietly contemplate
Mindfully meditate

And lustfully listen deeply to that which is beyond
The gnawing, incessant cries of grief
The painful shriek of the planet
The unending lament of Mother Nature . . .
Pausing
In a grace-filled moment of silence
I am able to hear the call of consciousness
The voice of knowing and wisdom that says
Lo aleicha hamelacha ligmor
It is not your duty to complete the task
V'lo ata ben chorim l'hivatil mimena
But neither are you free to avoid the call
That is in front of you.

All I can do is humbly accept the task
And simply do the next right thing.
All I can do is humbly accept the task
And gracefully do the next right thing.
Amen.

LOVE AND DEATH, MOURNING AND MEANING

AT THE GRAVE

Layered stories of a life history are told
Gently enveloping mourners
In a blanket of memory.
Prayers of lament elevate the soul heavenward
Drawn towards the gates of transformation.
With intentional concentration
Ropes lower a plain pine box into the ground
Burying body and coffin
In the belly of mother earth
As shoveled dirt eerily reverberates
Piercing the veil between this world
And the great beyond.
Dirge-like words of Kaddish are intoned
In muted voices
Aligning in hallowed resonance with all
Who have ever stood at the grave of a loved one.
Then with few words of soothing solace
Broken, bereaved and beckoned into an
Unknown valley of grief
Mourners file through supportive columns
Of community healing, hope and consolation.
The funeral is over
The journey of a lifetime comes to an end.
Now the rest of life awaits.
Such is the way of death.

To Harold—The Perennial Handyman

In honor of my father Harold Paull—read at his funeral

Way back when
We were always told
When you were young and bold
You told us you had been a general contractor
Mitchell Paul Construction
Right there on the business card
Named to honor your Dad
Mickey, Myron, Mitchell.
Of those days we only heard stories
Nostalgic longing for the inspired dreams
Of young man Harold.

But the Dad we saw was
The perennial handyman
Hammer, screwdriver, pliers
Never far from your skilled hands.
As children we watched in awe
Knowing you could fix anything large or small
Under the sink or behind a wall.
As adults we appreciate
Your resourcefulness, talent, creativity
And grew to admire the skill
The craft you worked so well.
By example, by encouragement
By annoying harassment

Certainly during our teenage years
You taught each of us
To wield the tools of the handyman
With comfort, confidence and competence
And you took pride in seeing
The natural outgrowth of your teaching
In the unique work benches
Tool collections and handyman projects
You inspired in your sons' homes
And even more, in their children
Who, like Zayde Harold
Can handle a hammer, nail, screwdriver
With creative ease.

And, of course, for all to see
The grand project of your life
Has been the beautiful home you created
For, and in partnership with, your beloved Rose
To live in comfort, convenience and beauty
Over the course of two decades
You envisioned and manifested major renovations
That transformed a simple
Two bedroom Laurentian cottage
Into a warm, inviting home
Filled with knick-knacks, Jewish books
Lots of tools, of course
Embellished with artwork
Produced by two old crows
The painters that you and my mother
Loved to call yourselves.

So the house has been built
All the projects you were to do in this lifetime
Are complete
No more lamps to fix
Not another hook to hang
The house is full
We are filled with the gifts of spirit
You've bequeathed to us.
We'll laugh and *kibitz*
Eat lots of cake
In your beautiful home
As you loved to do
And we'll remember and miss you dearly
Every time we reach for a hammer or screwdriver
Every time we start a new handyman project
And aspire to bring
More beauty to God's creation
As you taught us to do.
But today the hammers are silent
The pliers sit untouched
The saws and clamps rest
And we celebrate your life
Comfort each other and your wife
And remember how blessed we truly are
Knowing full well
Whenever we enjoy the corners of creativity
In your home or ours
You'll be there with us in spirit
The perennial handyman
You have always been.

Harold Palefsky Paull
Tzvi Hirsch ben Eidel Meir v'Shaindel
You've done your job and you've done it well!

Tehei Nishmato Tzurara B'Tzror HaHayyim
May his soul be welcomed back
to the Source of Life.

I Never Saw My Father Cry

You loved your father very deeply
A quiet man with a twinkle in his eye
His death touched you
In somnambulant places inside.
Day and night you said Kaddish for him
Remembering and integrating
His sweet legacy to you.
Yet in spite of being a fatherless son
Tears were unfamiliar to you
I knew you missed him very much
But not a visible tear was shed.
I never saw my father cry.

When your mother died
I asked you how you felt
Characteristically, with few words
Of self-reflection, you replied:
"She was a good mother
And I was a good son."
That was it, nothing more.
Burying and mourning his 86-year-old mother
I never saw my father cry.
Never, not once.

I was ten years old
When I reached into your sports jacket pocket
Ninety-two dollars after taxes your pay stub read.

Even then I understood your frustration
Trying to raise a family of five
Working day in, day out for
Your rich brother-in-law
With little recognition for your effort and time.
You knew humiliation, anger, probably shame
But if you felt despair, angst, depressed
You never let on
And even if you worked
Late-nights and second jobs
To make ends meet
I never saw my father cry.

Jobs came and went
Work promised, suddenly revoked
Deceived by a corrupt business partner
Fired for being a Jew
Companies, more than one
Gone bankrupt, sending you away.
Stable employment was never your strong suit
Selling cars, linoleum tiles, chalk boards
Maraschino cherries—red and green
Mail order business schemes
Driving taxi, even that was short-lived
So you went back, humiliated
To work for your brother-in-law
Because you believed you did
Whatever life required of you
And through it all
Struggles and disappointments

Failures and falling fortunes
Rarely were heard sighs, moans or groans
I never saw my father cry.

Surely love had its ups and downs
You and my mother loved each other
In spite of too much bickering
Quibbles, squabbles, kiss and make up
Start again only to apologize once more
Among the sixty years of loyal love
Surely there were betrayals
Unspoken secrets
Hurts, wounds of the heart
Moments of wondering why.
And yet in spite of cycles
Of affection and complaint
As partner to my mother
As a man in the world
Never was there a crack
In your dispassionate veneer
Was it authentic?
Or only your silent, secretive style?
You were after all a Scorpio
Either way, in matters of love
In affairs of the heart
I never saw my father cry
Never
Ever
Ever.

Then two years ago
You were called to the edge of the world beyond.
It was a breezy Florida night
Walking along and knocked over
By an unseeing driver
Bones broken, crushed
They say tire marks were engraved on your chest.
Barely able to move at first
Your sense of humor was the first to recover
Even as you lay in hospital for almost two months
Slowly re-learning to walk
To use your arms
To breath fully into bruised lungs
What a struggle it was to return from death's door
To choose life
To give us the gift of your presence
Almost two more years
Yet in spite of healing broken bones
And long-lingering aches and pains
You never railed at life.
And even more
Through it all
I never saw my father cry.

Instead, I saw you plod and persevere
Do each day what had to be done
Make a list
Attend to details one by one
From mundane to profane
Pick a number

Make someone laugh
Negotiate with carpenters and contractors
Listen to Kol Yisrael on your short-wave radio
Go to sleep
And start another day
And through it all
Seasons of summer, fall, winter, spring
Trips to Canadian Tire and Jean Coutu
In spite of the ordinary and the passing of time
I never saw my father cry.

Then three nights ago
Your breathed your last
Enjoying music
Being the trickster you were
Sharing laughs and pleasurable moments
With friends
Playful, prayerful
In your own inimitable style
Then you came home
Was it gastric distress, indigestion
Or your ever-present angina?
Either way, that fateful moment
You returned to the home you love
After taking care of yourself
As you did so well
You keeled over and died
Life ended as you knew it
And I never saw my father cry
I never saw my father cry.

Yesterday on a damp, cold Montreal afternoon
With your beloved family and friends around
We lowered a plain pine coffin into the earth
And said good-bye to your
Lifeless, ritually-purified body.
Sounds of tears were heard among us
Intermittent laughter and respectful silence
And deep sighs of painful loss
As the cold misty rain fell
We could sense your loving presence
Hear you *kibitzing* with those welcoming you
Into the world beyond
And as expected, through it all
I never saw my father cry.

Today your wife and sons
Daughters-in-law, grandchildren
And great-grandchild
Sit around and remember your life
We tell comical stories of your holy *hutzpah*
Recalling profound moments of wisdom
Everyday challenges you faced in silent courage
As was your style.

And while it's true
While you were alive
I never heard my father cry
I sit here and tears roll down my cheek
Because you died suddenly this week
And the only father I will ever have

Has gone from my life.
I won't hear your voice
On the other end of the phone
No more hugs
No gentle kiss on the forehead
As you always gave me
When arriving and departing.
Tears roll down my cheek
As I miss you right now
Amid the ever-present
Chatter and conversation of shiva.

And I cry
Deeply cry
Because you are dead
My Daddy, dead, gone from this world
To the realm of Spirit, of Presence
And I know with absolute certainty
From this day forth
I'll never see my father cry.
I'll never see my father cry.

SHIVA MOMENTS

Food platters and family matters
Laughter and tears
Angers, fears
Stories of life lived
Regrets of time lost
Eternal moments of memory
Woven together into a balm
To assuage the hurting heart
Release the untethered soul
And heal the empty hole
Unseen in the covered mirrors
Which hide the torn heart's anguish
As I languish
Grief-stricken
Yearning
Burning like a candle
In the dark night of the soul.

Praying with my weary body
I bind my memory of you into my arms
Between my eyes
As my heart, once again cries
Tears of love, loss and awakening.
Psalms of praise
Punctuate a mourner's daze
Shema Yisrael
Why the hell am I here?

Awake so early
Not in my bed
As you lie dead
Why?
I cry with a sigh
Standing
To enter the silence of prayer.

I greet the ancestors
And they comfort me
Unconditionally
Telling me they have welcomed you in death
For a moment I catch my breath
But then in the painful nuances
Of death and life renewed
I know it's not true
Embodied I will never see you again
Once more a wave of pain
Recalling you've breathed your last
This time of incarnation has past
Dead, buried, no longer even dying
Am I laughing or crying
Feeling the blessings of living
Reaching out
Forgiving
Deeply knowing the fullness of time
Seeing invisible patterns of the divine
Reflected in the candle light
That burns day and night.

In this prayer haze
As words jump off the page
I feel the echoes of older, younger generations
Meaningful interpretations
Punctuated and punctured once again
With lingering laments of sorrow and regret
The recognition of potentialities never to be met
Gifts bequeathed
Sacred moments now unclaimed
Was this death in vain?
Blessings harvested
Friends found and lost
Just how much did that box cost?
All these and more pass in my mind
In praying to the divine
Unfolding moment by moment
In this ever-present seven day vigil in your honor.
Until finally I pray for peace
Silently bend my knees
And sit down close to the ground
A prayed-out mourner am I
Not another tear to cry.

As the din definitely diminishes
And a majestic prayer finally finishes
Trembling, weary in my heart
Without hesitation, I slowly start
Momentarily mesmerized as I stand
Uttering cryptic words
Of a sacred chant

Yitkadal v'yitkadash
Lifetimes these words endure and last
Stuttering
Sputtering.

In dumb struck belief
There seems to be no relief
Until in the pause moments
I drop my fear and begin to hear
Praying through me
Ancient Aramaic incantations
Echoing patterns of the centuries
An indistinct primordial sound
Resounds deep inside
Claiming my birthright from days of old
An orphan in history
Awe-struck by this mystery
Of unseen connection
Of generations and generations
Children of fathers and mothers
Siblings of sisters and brothers
Woven into the warp and woof of life
Etched into eternity
Words older than time
Hallowing the divine
Magnifying
Sanctifying this moment
This life you have lived
This death I am discovering
This blessed Name I am uncovering

In this world and the world beyond
In the name of the one who makes peace
In the highest realms
In the human realms
In my aching heart
And in your awakening soul
And once more
Before another round of bagels and lox
Makes all my clothes tight
Down to my socks
Let us say—Amen!
Let us pray—Amen!

KADDISH ECHOES

Yitkadal v'Yitkadash
Magnified and sanctified
Enlarged, expanded and made holy
Shmei Rabba
The Great Name
The Grand Name
The many names of the One
Which one?
Whose great name?
What does it mean
To make a great name
Holy, larger?
How can I do that?
Just by uttering
An ancient Aramaic formula
That my father
   my grandfather
   my great-grandfather
   my great great-grandfather
And his ancestors
Uttered over and over?
Is that grand?
Is that holy?
Is that meaningful?
Healing
Transformative
Profound?

These words seem to resonate
From this world
To the world beyond
Piercing the veil
Of time and space.

But what is the Great Name?
Who is the Great Name?
What is the Profound Hearing?
Is it the Nameless One?
The Infinite One?
That is blessed   *yitbarakh*
  praised   *v'yishtabakh*
  glorified   *v'yitpoar*
  elevated   *v'yitromam*
  extolled   *v'yitnaseh*
  honored   *v'yithallal*
  lauded   *v'yihaleh*

How can I evoke
A Name I know not?
Am I praising
  adulating
  adoring
  worshipping
  beautifying
  elevating
  lauding
The Holy Name
The One beyond any blessings and hymns?

But which Name?
And why? And why not?
Not my name
Not my father's name
So who is that One
Who will bring
Abundant peace from Heaven?
And when I stand
Pronouncing these archaic words
Am I really able to evoke
Abundant peace
Cosmic harmony
For all Israel
For all the world
Do my words have power?
Does my grief find consolation in these words?
Am I powerless to connect
With the realm of the dead?
In this time of powerlessness
These ancient words
Yitkadal, v'Yitkadash
I cry out
To open my heart
To remember your presence
To touch your heart
In there peace in all the world?
Is there peace in my heart?
Is there peace between me and my brothers?
Between Isaac and Ishmael?
Yitkadal, v'Yitkadash

Make holy my suffering
My longing, my sorrow
May the Name of the Holy One be present.

To Dad—
A Post-Mortem Appreciation

Everywhere I turn these days
I am repeatedly reminded of how well
You taught me to do life
To negotiate my way
Through the ever-changing
Maze of daily intricacies
People, places, things
In a unique and succinct style
Permeated by humor and *hutzpah*
Patience and passion
Determination and decency.

From you I have learned
A multitude of many matters
Like how to paper a dirty toilet seat
Or to ask to speak with someone's supervisor
And gently cajole them
To meet my administrative needs
And, of course, to remember
To warm my car on cold winter mornings.
For all of these, and many more
I am ever-grateful
Daily, moment by moment
I now appreciate the legacy
Of functional skills you have transmitted
Undeniably indispensable as I

Navigate my way through mid-life
In this uncertain age of post-millennial stress.

And yet, in the wake of your sudden death
To my surprise and consternation
I now see with a growing sense of clarity
How I have yet to master with maturity
Qualities of spirit and human virtues
You taught only by silent example
In between the pauses and sighs
Of your own struggles:
A quiet certitude about life's upsets
A non-religious faith in final outcome
Patience, persistence and a silent, unbroken trust.

And now that you are dead and buried
The learning that remains, I must do on my own.
Perhaps guided by your other-worldly Presence
I can now harvest inherited seeds
Never before noticed
Watered intermittently by erratic
Night-time tears of longing
And fertilized by earth thrown upon your coffin
Just weeks ago, in the dead of winter.
And so, missing you as deeply as I do, my father
Even if I warmed up my car
This cold winter morning
Sunny days and springtime of rebirth
Still feel a long way off, a long way off.

The Last Kaddish

Eleven months have passed
No fanfare
No grand ritual moment
Barely a whimper
And a sigh
Followed by the ongoing
Perennial question
Why did you have to die?
Because your time was up
And now
According to the wise advice
Of Rabbi Moses Isserles
Who said parents
Only get limited not maximum
Time in Gehenna
Whatever that is
Eleven months after we buried you
On a freezing cold day
Today, with the last
Of autumn leaves
Making their earthbound descent
Today
The streaming waves
Of the Kaddish channel
Go silent
My status as a mourner
Among the community of Israel

Among the community of humanity
Changes suddenly
And forever more
Almost as suddenly
As my life changed
The day you died
And today
Like everyday
The past eleven months
I am a fatherless child
I am a son
Without a father
A little boy
Standing alone
Without his Daddy
I am a man
Orienting myself in the world
With only a compass of memory and legacy
Flying by the seat of his pants
Today as I utter these words
Yitkadal v'Yitkadash
Shmei Rabbah
One last time
As a mourning child
I will praise the Great Name
The One that helped me
Guided and healed me
Throughout these months
Of mourning
And when I say

Yehei shmei rabbah mevorakh
L'olam u'lamei almayah
I shall look upwards
To the supernal worlds
Stretching through all time and space
And contemplate the mysteries
Of life, death, love and loss
Once more
As I've done each and every day
Since you died
And for a moment
There will be a twinge
A subtle heart-opening
Soul-stirring
Mind-meandering
Kaddish connecting
Moment
A momentary passing visit
With my father
As I praise, adulate
Adorn and bless my God
Thanking God
For Presence
For Peace
In my life
And in the life of all humanity
And as the words end
Eleven months of Kaddish saying
Have passed
The Kaddish channel goes silent

And I now know
I will never be the same
Life will have changed forever.

My Dad Owned a Studebaker

Forty years ago
My Dad owned a Studebaker
Shining and bright
He brought it home
The first brand-new car he ever owned
Elegant and black on the outside
A plush soft blue interior
We were all so proud
Driving around in that Studebaker
I always remember
Dad at the wheel
Rolling down the windows
His left elbow and arm gracefully
Hovering out the window
As if it were today
I can see the hair on his arm
Being blown by the breeze
Softly
Gently
Like that plush blue interior.
Driving at the wheel
He seemed to radiate such confidence
A mastery that was both mythic and magical.

It was 1964
I was coming into my own
A teenage boy

A middle age Dad
A new car
How sweet it was
Even if I spent my teenage years
Locked in my room
Alone, lonely and confused
Dad and mom both worked
My older brother
Long ago had not much use for me
My younger brother
Well he was a cute kid
Everyone said that
But I was in my own world
Lost in the onslaught
Of ever-present adolescent angst
But every so often
Like ever other happy suburban family
Of baby-boomer children
We'd all go for a ride
In that Studebaker

That, like all of us
Aged slowly
Aged quickly
By the time I was 17
In 1968
John Kennedy
Robert Kennedy and
Martin Luther King were all dead
And I was ready

To learn to drive
That old, beat up Studebaker
Dad now had a new car
A shining 1968 Oldsmobile Delmont '88
Like many a man of his generation
He liked a car
That drove like a boat
I got to drive Mom's car
That old Studebaker
My very first car
Pushing 100,000 miles
I could still hit over 70 miles per hour
Speeding home from my girlfriend's
Past my curfew
After a night of heavy petting
I remember her well
Making out in that Studebaker
With that special girl
But she eventually dumped me
New girlfriends get old fast
And eventually we had to dump
That old Studebaker
Too old to maintain.

High school ended
College adventures began
For a while I even owned a Volkswagen Beetle
Not too much room for making out
Girlfriends came and went
Some more often than others

Dad liked big cars
And when it was time for another one
Reluctantly at first, he bequeathed to me
That big old Oldsmobile Delmont 88
And with whats her name, my live-in lover
We drove off to California
In our funky old Olds
In search of spirit, adventure, graduate school.
Well, as to be expected
One day
Well past 140,000 miles
That Oldsmobile Delmont 88
Ended up in a junk heap
As did the relationship with what's her name
More girlfriends
More cars
And I did graduate from graduate school.

As Dad got older
And gas prices climbed
Over $1.00 a gallon
He drove Hondas
Seeing big fat Dad in a little Honda
Seemed funny at first
But, like the Studebaker
He drove each new car
With a real sense of pride
We used to say
Dad had four children
Three sons and a car

Even at the end of his life
After a car knocked him down
Leaving an 83-year-old man
Hospitalized for months
He walked again
Settled the accident claim
And proudly bought himself a new car
A bright red Honda
He drove to his very last day
Got out of the car
Not feeling very well
Walked into the house
And dropped dead soon after
No more Dad
No more cars
No more old Studebaker
Just a picture of the
Shiny black old Studebaker
Sitting on my desk
Sitting on my desk
Reminding me of how it was
Forty years ago
Reminding me how
I miss my Dad.

WHEN SHE WAS OLD
MY MOTHER WORE PURPLE

After completing sitting shiva for my mother
"Purple" Rose – Rose Geiger Paull.

With appreciation to "When I Am an Old Woman I
Shall Wear Purple" by Jenny Joseph

When she was old my mother wore purple.

Oldest child of newly married immigrant parents
As a young girl and throughout her early years
My mother had striking jet-black hair
Sometimes worn long
Sometimes worn above her ears
She was beautiful, radiant, charming and talented
Dancing, singing
And no doubt verbally precocious
Confident and creative
Clearly the apple of her father's eye

And when she was old my mother wore purple.

At ten years of age her radiant smile
Was turned to tears by tragedy
Her father, a merchant of means
Photos showing the image of a well-dressed man
Handsome and proud

Was killed instantly in a car accident
On a summer day
That changed the destiny
Of my mother's life forever
Oldest of three children
Daughter of a thirty-three-year-old widow
Amidst the grief and trauma
No one would have ever guessed that

When she was old my mother would wear purple.

Raised by her mother and divorced aunt
Five children in a home
Filled with love, stern discipline and little money
My mother learned frugality, loyalty
Respect of *Yiddishkeit* and the value of family.
She grew up in Ste. Agathe
A small town country girl
Attended Baron Byng High School
Perhaps like a fish out of water
Still excelling in her grades
At the top of her class.

And when she was old my mother wore purple.

A hotelkeeper's daughter
She graciously attended to her mother
Like a surrogate husband
And acquired a rich tapestry
Of functional life skills

Navigating her way through a range
Of relationships and situations
Learning to organize the innumerable details
Of hotel reservations
Cooking continuously for fifty
To one hundred and more
And always embellishing a dining room table
With class and beauty
These survival skills lasted a lifetime
To the very end of her days.

And when she was old my mother wore purple.

Married to my father Harold
Creating a six decade long partnership
Together they brought three sons into the world
Lived in Ste. Agathe, Ottawa and Montreal
Wherever they moved setting up a beautiful home
Tasteful, aesthetic and welcoming to all
Especially at times of great Hanukah parties
Meaningful Passover Seders
And sweet, comforting Shabbat dinners.
In the prime of her life
Still sporting jet-black hair
There was still hardly a clue that
When she was old my mother would wear purple.

Years and years as a travel agent
The telephone sometimes seemed
Permanently attached to her ear

Capable, competent, radiating confidence
Covering up that insecure, fatherless country girl
Deep inside
Rose the travel agent
Charmed and wooed all she met
With her intelligence, wit and
Gregarious extraverted nature
Ever-professional by day
Wife and mother of three by night
Sister, sister-in-law, aunt, cousin
Long before the age of feminism
This was Rose Paull, my multi-talented mother

And when she was old my mother wore purple.

When the grandchildren came along
Bubby Rose emerged
Delightfully loving and caring for
Her children's children
Each of them uniquely special to her heart
And as her hair turned from black to gray
She experimented with colors
Brunette, platinum, brown
But no one would have suspected that

When she was old my mother would wear purple.

My mother loved the fresh air of Ste. Agathe
With crisp Laurentian Mountain winter snows
Perfectly mild, verdant summer days

All too brief, with early fall coming on
In late August.
Accompanied by her beloved Harold
They laughed and played
Painted, entertained friends
Watched television and listened to music
Shopped for groceries and went to synagogue
Finding many ways of enjoying rewards
Of retired life
Sharing the challenges of aging.
She began to blossom into her full self
Surrounded by flowers, birds,
Large vats of strawberry jam
And visits from friends, relatives
Children and grandchildren.

And when she was old my mother wore purple.

One day, one hot summer's day
My mother's life was transformed
She took a walk on the wild side
Daring to experiment
She dyed her gray hair
Not red, not blond, not black, not silver
Not lightly tinted, not a rinse
But yes, purple!
Close to eighty years old
My mother dyed her white hair purple
Purple hair on an old lady
Who walked with a cane

A new chapter of her life had begun.

When she was old my mother wore purple.

With purple hair my mother became
The belle of the mall
The talk of the town
The lady with purple hair
And a purple cane
Purple earrings and necklaces
Purple sweaters and shawls
And of course purple hats
And when she went to synagogue
She covered herself with a purple *talis*.
They stopped and talked
They stopped and gawked
Yes, it became plain for all to see

When she was old my mother wore purple.

In her old age
Body ravaged by Parkinson's
Hobbling with a walker
Decked out in her purple finery
Purple hair and an all-knowing smile
She became a model of aging with grace
Dignity intact in spite of debility
They all knew her as Purple Rose
The one who wrote poetry with her fountain pen
Worked on her computer

Still made jams every spring
And offered her wisdom to all
Solicited and unsolicited
Yes at every moment
It was clear for all to see

When she was old my mother wore purple.

She lived life fully in the face of loss
Loving as well as she could
Laughing, learning
Curious to discover the world around her
She was always reading a new book
Even as her eyes failed
Singing in the choir
Going on outings when she could
Ready to keep exploring
She even had a new boyfriend
In the last months of her life
And sent her grandchildren Hanukah presents
Just days before she died
And to the very last

When she was old my mother wore purple.

Nine years to the day my father died
My mother breathed her last
Aware that her time come
Seeing her father approaching
From the world beyond

Knowing my father too
Waited for her patiently, loyally
The journey was about to transition
She'd done her job
It was time to move on after a long colorful life

And when she was old my mother wore purple.

At the memorial tribute
Held in the assisted living community
Where she resided the last eight years of her life
Old women gathered with their
Canes, walkers and wheelchairs
So many wearing purple in her honor.
At her funeral we all donned purple clothes
And purple ribbons as a testament to her life
An acknowledgement of her legacy to each of us
Who knew with absolute certainty that

When she was old my mother wore purple.

Today I have ended the time of sitting shiva
My mother is dead and buried
I won't see her face to face
Decked out in purple finery
With flaming purple hair
Even though I will hold her dearly in my heart
I won't hear her loving voice on the phone
Nor read her loving birthday greetings
Written with purple ink

Sometimes I'll dress in white and black
My favorite colors
Or yellow, blue, green, red
I hardly ever wear brown
And sometimes I'll see others wearing purple
Reminding me of my colorful mom
But no matter what I will miss her dearly
And remember that

When she was old my mother wore purple.

Now she's dead,
She's a disembodied spirit
Who has left me a living legacy
For that I will always be grateful
I'll remember her many attributes
Charismatic qualities, characteristics and gifts
And come what may
I will always be proud of
My mother's creative courage
Her unique and holy *hutzpah*
And I will always be able to say that

When she was old my mother wore purple.

Purple Rose I love you
I miss you dearly
But come what may, as I age
As my beard and hair become silver
Wherever I go from this point on

However my life story will unfold
I'll always remember and tell everyone that

When she was old my mother wore purple.
When she was old my mother wore purple.

FOR HAROLD AND ROSE— AN UNVEILING POEM

Standing here, before your gravestones
I am a parentless child
Not a little boy without my mommy and daddy
Nor a young man, glad to be away from my
parents
Not even a middle-aged man
Seeing the road ahead before my eyes
Today I am in the second half of my life
Closer to the day of my death
Than to the day of my birth.
With no living parents or grandparents
I stand at the top of the generational chain
Knowing I have been given gracious gifts of spirit
And a lasting legacy of a life of meaning
As well as love, family and
A sometimes skewed
Sometimes inspired set of values
All of which have prepared me to navigate
The remaining years of the journey I call my life
Without my parents alive,
But with your presence ever-present.

Standing here, seeing your
Names and dates of birth and death
Etched into marble
Reminding me that in this sacred cemetery space

Euphemistically called
Mount Pleasant Memorial Park
Your once-weary and worn out bodies are buried
Covered in the holy linen shrouds
Of Jewish sacred burial tradition
Delicately placed in plain pine caskets
Beneath the moist Quebec earth.

In the wake of the inevitability of death
Your individual and coupled stories survive
In the hearts and minds
Of each of us gathered here today
Both of you oldest children of immigrant parents
Born prior to the Great Depression
The long and multifaceted drama of life lived
Lasting for each of you almost nine decades
Spanning the twentieth
Into the twenty-first century
In your lifetime
You witnessed the manifestation
Of technological wonder
From the advent of radio and telephone,
Television and microwave cooking
To the miracle of personal computers
Mobile telephones and the now-ubiquitous
Internet and information superhighway.

The profound panoply of life experience
Filled with challenge and changing circumstances
Lives of love and laughter, tears and pain

Highlights and lowlights
Family and tradition, travel and travail
Peppered with patience and persistence
In the face of it all
Varied and variegated stories, told and retold
Some secrets never-told
All form the essential elements of the eternal gifts
Forever etched into
The deepest dimensions of my being
The foundation and bedrock of my psyche
Benevolently bequeathed to me as my parents
For better or worse, for now and forever more.

And on this day, I humbly honor your memory
Continuing to transform
My own mourning into meaning
Heart-filled longing into a holy legacy
Assiduously aspiring to heal
Historical hurts of the heart
Transforming in quantum leaps and bounds
Oh so many layers
Archaic residues of oft-told traumas
And the dialectical dizzying dramas
Of our family life.

And out of all these mental meanderings
And emotional machinations
I know my tender heart that has
Loved and been loved
Feeling fully imbued with the magic and mystery

Of all that you have bestowed
Upon and within me
And though as an orphaned adult child I feel sad
At times lonely, and missing you in my daily life
Missing phone conversations, and empathic
caring
Saturated with unquestioned concern
About my life
And my wife, my children and
My hopes and dreams
Today in front of your tombstones
I am filled with the blessings
You have bequeathed to me
And I am unquestionably aware of
The lasting legacy you have left behind
I feel blessed and grateful that you
Rose Geiger Paull
and you Harold Palefsky Paull
have been my parents
May your names be etched forever
Into the eternal memory of our people
May your names be etched forever
Into the eternal memory of our family
And may your souls
Be bound up in the bond of eternal life
And may your souls return
To the Source of Life
Tehei nishmatem tzrura b'ztror ha-hayyim.

YIZKOR VISION

In the crisp autumn air
I went to say
Yizkor prayers today
One of those holy days
Four times a year
We gather in community
Mourners threaded by
Memories of heart and mind
A direct line to loved ones
In the world beyond.
Four times a year
Ever since the Crusades
When mega-death
Demanded memorialization
Jews have said Yizkor
Remembrance
To honor, remember, elevate
Souls of dead loved ones.
It was fascinating
As I looked around the room
The synagogue was packed
Death, after all is said and done
Is a popular attraction
Yet to my surprise
Through the vision of my eyes
There was hardly
An adult in the room

Those saying Yizkor for parents
I saw on their faces
Pain and love
Of little boys and girls
Lost, lonely
Crying for Mommys and Daddys
Those remembering dead brothers and sisters
They too were pained children
A little brother
Reaching for his older sister's hand
A little girl, standing next to her sister
Both of them wondering why
Their little brother died
And even that man
Saying Yizkor for his dead wife
For a brief moment
Looked like a lost child
Unsure if someone
Will ever be there
To light the way
So many children
Being cleansed by their tears.
In an instantaneous moment
Of infinite time
Something changed
Reciting the *el maleh rachamim*
In mournful dirge
Suddenly the windows opened
Souls ancient, eternal, transcendent
Seemed to stream into the space

Visible on everyone's face
Each lost child
Seemed to be comforted
Through soul's presence
Our prayers invited
A heavenly congregation
Of wondrous, watching, wise beings
Ancestral guides
Mommys, Daddys
Bubbys, Zaydes from the other side
Loved ones who walk with us
Day and night
Easing pain, loneliness and fright
And somehow in the afterglow
Of so many souls
Beckoned and present
As our praying moments
Softly came to an end
Each face, man, woman and child
Looked a little older
A little wiser
Deepened in the interior channels
Of heart and soul
Walking with dignity
The mourners path
Of our ancient sages
Deepened in knowing
Death and loss
Come what may
Are truly and evermore

Interwoven into
The mystery and the enigma
Of being alive
Of being human.

MIDLIFE, PARENTING AND MARRIAGE

THE PREGNANT FATHER PONDERS

No kicking in the belly
Or late night hunger surges
Remind my body of your immanent birth
In my life.

Sure I have gained a few pounds
Too many cookies eaten to silence
The din of anxiety.

Though another's body, another's loins
Birth you into the world
I stand pregnant inside
Readying to catch you as you land in my arms.

And I shall call you Son, Daughter
And you shall know me as Abba-Daddy.

Never, ever can I remove the empty scar
Of orphaned life.
All the knowing of time and mind
Can't fill the wound, nor answer why.
I only know in this pregnant moment of time
Your destiny and mine are being called to meet.

You, the Orphan I shall call my Child.
I, the Pregnant Father
Praying to be worthy to love you
In the fullness of time.

Praying to birth from within me
Compassionate wisdom, patience, and love
Abundant energy, humor and a gentle spirit.

That I may respond to your cries
And fulfill this destiny we have created
Aeons ago, in the womb of eternal time.*

* Published in *Adoption Today*, July 2002, p. 33

Tiring Thoughts at Bedtime

As midnight silence descends
I tuck my bedraggled body into the
multitude of messy unmade covers upon my bed
and finally pause for a meditative moment
to feel the drowsiness in my head.
As day ends it dawns upon me
just how exceptionally exhausted
woeful, weary and
terribly tired I am.

Why is that, I wonder?

Is it because the subtle
but seemingly ever-present
hell-realms of healing
have unleashed
miniature monsters of mental meandering
unbridling habitual habits
Of rampant rumination over
irascible and irrepressible recollections of
pathetic pleasures of the past
that once seemed holy and are now
uncovered as unholy alliances
dangerous dalliances of deception
which cannot and do not
and probably never did
replenish the spirit?

Or perhaps the body is terribly tired
and fantastically fatigued
because daily demands
relentlessly require
and involuntarily evoke
every accessible ounce of energy
leaving preciously rare resources available
for occasional fitful moments
of pleasure or ecstasy
and thus I am left languishing in
daily depletion and deficiency
if not outright damnation?

Maybe.
Maybe not.

Either way, I think I am tired
because it was a busy weekend
and two rowdy and rambunctious kids
a sick wife
a messy house
a chaotic bank book
bad weather
too much chocolate and coffee
and lack of sleep and exercise
take their toll on
body
mind
spirit.

And besides all of the above
absolutely absurd aspects of
everyday happenstance
at the mid-century markings of mid-life
my mercurial mind meanders
into deep recesses of past and future
memories and visions
of childhood and death
creatively contemplating
simultaneous and secretive
corners of clarity and confusion
karma and chaos
in instantaneous flashes of inspired insight
and I wonder if I am
wise or foolish
blessed or cursed
benign or a bloody bastard
a receptor of mystical vision
or starkly and simply insane.

Somehow such thoughts
experienced in fleeting holographic moments
of cosmic in breath, out breath
squeezed in between parental interludes
at baby's bath time
and excessive email
all leave me tentatively tethered
teasingly tantalized
inching everyday

towards wholeness or emptiness
cosmic void or karmic vapidity.

No wonder I am tired.

Now stop writing poetry
close the light
and go to sleep.

Oh yeah
and by the way
don't forget to say prayers.

From a Father to a Son
In Honor of Your Bar Mitzvah

Baby boy birthed into the world
First-born son of mother and father
Destined to become
A full-standing member of the Jewish people
Inheritor of the ancient religion of Judaism
Creator of the community
Of twenty-first century Jews

Slowly, day-by-day
Baby boy grows up
Learns to walk
Learns to talk
Meandering the halls of
Germantown Jewish Centre
Discovering the rhythms of Jewish life
Holy days, Shabbat
Celebrations of the sacred seasons of Jewish time

Slowly, week-by-week
Boy child grows up
Learns to read, to write
To sing and pray
In the language of the ancestors
Hebrew, holy hebrew
Lashon Ha-Kodesh.

Yigdal—he shall grow mighty
Once a four pound, four ounce preemie
Yigdal, grows mighty
A good student
   athlete
   friend
   son
   brother
Year-by-year
Yigdal, grows mighty
And approaches the vestibule of puberty
Preparing to pass through the mysterious portal
Into the sacred realms of Jewish life
Slowly, methodically
But very definitely
Boy morphing into man
Embarks upon the mythical trek
To become
A Bar Mitzvah!
A what?
A Bar Mitzvah?
What exactly is that?
Son of the Commandments
A man of Mitzvoth
A mensch among Jewish men
Like his father, grandfathers
Great-grandfathers before him
Thirteen years old
Able to be counted in a minyan

But what is a Bar Mitzvah?
What is this holy event?
This sacred tribal gathering
We are here to celebrate?
Is this only the final culmination of
A dizzying carousel of
Logistics beyond logical expectations
Parties and planning
Invitations and menus
Guest lists and to do lists?
Is Bar Mitzvah any more than the
Serendipitous or perhaps fortunate result of
Parents planning into the wee small hours
Of the night
As the young man sharpens his voice
Agonizes over music and melodies
Speeches and the far reaches of understanding
Torah and tradition in our time?

Then . . . finally . . .
The day has arrived!
It's Bar Mitzvah time here in Mount Airy!
Let the show begin!
Aardvarks disembark
Get on the bus
Leave the driving to us
Here comes the shul
Here comes the Bar Mitzvah boy
Today I am a party favor
Today I am a monogrammed blue kippah!

Today I am a man!
Is that all there is to a Bar Mitzvah?

What does it mean to become a man?
A woman can change an embryo to a boy
But what changes a boy to a man?
Answer: walking the sacred pilgrimage
Towards becoming a Bar Mitzvah!
Bar Mitzvah - a time to read Torah
To study, to learn, to give a speech
To daven, to serve as a leader of prayer
To participate in the community of Jewish men
To participate in the community
Of Jewish men and women
Bar Mitzvah - a time of deepening
A time of learning and growing
And knowing and showing
Of praying and staying the course
Of course.
Bar Mitzvah is not only the end of boyhood
Talking to girls, not only boys
Giving away your old toys
Bequeathing outgrown beanie babies to your sister
Growing to an extra large size
Or maybe a man's small?
Is he really that tall?
Clearly, right before our eyes
The boy-child is dying off
The little boy is no longer

A young man is being resurrected
A second birth, he grows mighty
Minute by minute
Watch out, here comes another growth spurt!

As a Bar Mitzvah, you have begun
The journey of a lifetime
To become who you truly are
A rite of passage to a fuller you
An adventure in search of full self.
A voyage to strange new worlds
To discover who exactly is Yigdal
Who is your God?
Who are your people?

But wait!
None of the great Jews of antiquity
Had Bar Mitzvahs
Not Abraham or Moses
Not Solomon, David or Jonathan
Not Rabbi Akiva
So what is this journey?
How can this rite of passage
Birth the soul of a Jewish boy?
Abraham journeyed through the desert
Called to be father of a nation
Moses journeyed in the wilderness
Called to be a leader
The Israelite tribes

Journeyed from slavery to freedom
Called to become a holy nation
And a kingdom of priests.

And you, Yigdal
Bar Mitzvah boy
You now begin your journey
To grow into the mighty person
You are called to be.
At thirteen, the Rabbis taught
The *yetzer ha-tov* enters a person
The desire to act from beneficence is born
And you are now given the opportunity
To nourish and grow your *yetzer ha-tov*
Your sense of what is right for the world
In which we live today

At thirteen, Bezalel, the sacred architect
Designed the Holy Mishkan
And you, Bar Mitzvah boy, are called to journey
Towards the fullness of your creativity.

At thirteen, Avraham smashed
The idols of his father Terah
And you, Bar Mitzvah boy, are called to find
What is your own truth
Your own God.

At thirteen, Esav and Yaakov
Each went their ways

One into idolatry
One into service of God.
And you, ben Simcha v'Geela Rayzel
Are now called into your tribal community
To live a life of Torah,
Avodah and *Gemillut Hasadim*
However you understand that to be
To learn and study the ancient
Wisdom lineage of the past
And to make it your own
To find your own ways of wrestling with God.
However you understand God to be
To find your ways of serving this world
A world at war
A world in which there is richness and poverty
A world where there are haves and have-nots
And you—Bar Mitzvah boy
Have begun the journey of self-discovery
To find your own voice
Your own song
Your own spirit
To take your place
In the community of Jews
In this wonder-filled community of Mount Airy
In this nation, at this time in history
And in the world community
Which desperately cries out for healing
And today, on this sacred day in your life
Your parents,your grandparents,
In this world and the world beyond

Your aunts and uncles
Your cousins and friends welcome you
Into our sacred tribal gathering
Blessing you with our love
Proud of how you have grown
These past thirteen years
And knowing
Wherever you go
Whatever you do
Wherever you travel
Whomever you love
We will love you
We will always welcome you
As a member of this ever-changing
Family of tribes
Gathered around the holy of holies
Gathered together in God's Name.

Happy Bar Mitzvah!
The journey awaits my son
Travel wisely, gently
Courageously, faithfully
Thanks for giving all of us the opportunity
To stand together with you
And welcome you into our family of tribes
United as one.
Baruch Atta Adonai Eloheinu Ruakh Ha-Olam
Shecheyanu v'kiyemanu, v'higiyanu la'zman ha'zeh.
Blessed be the Holy One who has brought us all
To this most auspicious and sacred moment.

ODE TO A SEVEN-YEAR-OLD TOMBOY

Boy-girl with short-cropped hair
Long eyelashes
Strong muscles
Proudly shown
Deep erratic feelings
And a baseball cap
Worn backwards
Well-placed, intentional
Just in case
Anyone doubts who
You really are.

Whoever you are
Whoever you will be
You will always be loved by me.

IMAGES OF MY LIFE
REFLECTED IN THE FIRE

In honor of Yigdal's 14th birthday party

i like to sit in front of the fireplace
watching the ambient glow of embers
dancing flames
hearing crackling wood
exuding warmth
radiating light
soothing the spirit
it's so rare to sit in front of the fireplace
sipping deliciously warmed
flavored coffee
out of my favorite mug
listening to contemplative music
piano and flute interwoven in an embrace
punctuated only by
the chiming grandfather clock
reminding me
this exact moment
this time
this rhyme
is so perfect
so profoundly delightful
as i sit in front of the fireplace
thinking of my day.
seemed like hours ago
cleaning chaos and clutter

on miles and miles of
dirty kitchen counters
with kids crying, whining
fighting with each other
taking turns
dramatizing
the trauma of the sibling project
he said, she said
and she said
he started it
and when he laughed
she yelled louder
and said she wasn't yelling
she was screaming
and why was i laughing
and then the phone rang
it always does
and it rang and rang
because no one could find it
hidden among papers and piles, pieces of life
all leftover from yesterday's birthday party
and what a party it was!

twenty-two 13-14-year-olds
boys and girls
but the girls went home at midnight
would you want to sleep over
on the floor
in a pack of fart-worshipping
burping, wrestling, tv-addicted 14-year-olds

running outside
playing basketball at 2 o'clock in the morning
half naked in ten degree temperatures?
Lord of the Flies had nothing on this pack
of 14-year-old boys
who were determined to see dawn
just as determined as i was
to clean up the mess
leftovers
pizza
cake
ice cream
soda
hot chocolate
lasagna—lots of lasagna leftovers
apparently eating pizza is cool
eating lasagna is not
peanuts
pretzels
chips
cookies
and more
all needed to quell the
hungry masses
who seemed to graze or devour
every hour on the hour.
in the wee small hours of the night
all seemed under control
until the 4:00 AM munchies hit
and my de-clutter cleanup

was again deluged
this time with
boxes of cereal opened and spilled
milk splotches
crackers
cheese
and more
until i chased them all away
like i would banish a pack of mice
eating the trails of their crumbs and leftovers
"go back downstairs and go to sleep please"
i pleaded and contorted
and finally in exasperation
exiled them all
to the underworld basement
saturated with teenage testosterone
and adolescent attitude.

exhausted and weary
i left the kitchen
and carried my weary body off to bed
to get a few hours of sleep
until the morning wake up call.
i was on once again for breakfast
supervising the inmate population
avoiding rioting, conflagration
or any other attempts at whatever
consistently interspersed and infused with
hormonal eruption, self-destruction, vandalism
and other forms and configurations

of random chaos
before my sleep-deprived eyes
i could see a gang of 14-year-old boys
simultaneously groggy and giddy
laughing at the re-telling of
last night's fart stories
all ravenously hungry
some slurping cereal
others making their own eggs
painting my kitchen
emulating Picasso in a frenzy
while i am like the cat in the hat
doing a balancing dance
of pots and pans
attending to multiple requests for
more food and drink
while waking up last minute stragglers
and doing a damage assessment survey
from the night of adventure
finding pieces of broken remnants
minor in scope
major in irritation
do i try to teach lessons
in responsibility and moral foundation
or cut my losses
be grateful nothing more was destroyed
even if the television
fell off the table
"it's not my fault"
was the immediate battle cry

"well, fix it!" was my parental retort
someone among these technological savvy boys
able to handle this one
so we made it through that hoop
and slowly sent the pack
off one-by-one
to basketball practice
let the coach deal with them
so i can wind my way
through the debris
and end last night's party
and start today's agenda
a fairly simply one
to balance the bankbook
of missing deposits
unknown ATM withdrawals
vaguely etched checks
to chiropractors
cleaning ladies
book stores
bead stores
shoe stores
too many credit card companies to count
where is that extra $500
i know it was here yesterday
or last week
or was that last month?
but if i try
and calculate
computate

compute
dilute
change
rearrange
add
subtract
detract
reflect
and reject
i know
i think
i am 100% certain
i can
finally
absolutely
undeniably
get this bank book to balance
almost
a bit more
there's a paper on the floor
if only
now
maybe
maybe . . .
yes!
yes!
it's done!
so now i can finally
get around
to those six loads of laundry

desperately awaiting my attention
oh! here's the phone!
maybe i can even
find the top of my desk
as i finally begin
to prepare for another week
of classes
clients
conversations
images
visions
revisions
and all those other appointments
dentist
therapist
psychic
healer
wheeler
dealer
and everyone else
who needs me to slow down
take it easy
breathe
sit by the fireplace
and hang out.

oh yeah! fireplace!
oh! fireplace!
shit! the fire's gone out!
the music stopped

coffee is cold
oh well!
relaxation is over.
oh well!
think i'll take a shower
and go to bed
tomorrow is another day.

For the Flower Essence Lady

There are no simplistic solutions to my life
No potions, lotions, mixes or quick fixes
Which will undo, re-screw or even re-new
The kinks and quandaries
Conundrums and quirks
Which seem to make me me.

I know that if I could, I probably would
And maybe even should
Be more mellow and polite
And gentle and light
Smooth at the edges
Tranquil, not pushing the ledges
Be the kind of guy I am simply just not.

Sorry if it's true
Even if I may disappoint you
But there are no simplistic solutions to my life.
But let's face it, if there were
Would you still be my wife?

HAZARDS OF DOMESTIC LIFE: A LAMENT

I wandered through our most beautiful home
Stepping over hoards of clutter and congestion
Clothes, newspapers, old mail
Pathetically piled on counter tops and tables
Empty garbage bags
Strewn across the floor
Random, chaotic
Disdainfully dropped anywhere, everywhere
Silently tiptoeing my way
Through the debris
Hungry inside
I wonder
Can I find solace in food?

Opening the fridge door
I am greeted by a collage
Of plastic containers
Three of them fall at my feet
Revealing a coagulation
Of more kitchen chaos
Layers of leftovers
Opened bottles
Leaking Tupperware
Rotting vegetables
Nothing new
Nothing out of the ordinary
Nothing here to fill

The emptiness I feel inside.
 I close the fridge
And walk over to a mirror
Staring at my face
I see my solitary struggle
To create order and beauty
Serenity and safety
In an aesthetically analgesic
Home environment
But it's too painful to stare any longer
I move on.

As I walk out of the kitchen
I notice the front door
It's ajar, unlocked
I am unprotected from the world
Vulnerable
Victim to the changing vicissitudes
Of peri-menopausal memory
And other priorities
Okay we live in suburbia
Not the inner city
Maybe it's my urban paranoia
I thought doors were to be locked
Windows to be closed
Little things like this
Taken for granted
I guess not
Not in this home anyway.
Hungry and vulnerable

I feel the emptiness deepen
I am searching for something else
What is it, I wonder?
Exactly how did I get here anyway?

Willfully walking
Up the green carpeted stairs
I tryingly traverse
The three-tiered highway
Consisting of coagulates of
More chaos, clutter and congestion
Piles of kids' clothing
Junk mail, urgent announcements
Toys, ties, teddy bears
Slippers, shoes
And of course
Single socks
Lots of single socks
Adorning the carpeted floor
Like leopard spots
This place reminds me
Of the road to Baghdad
After the Gulf War
And I'm a weary soldier
Pondering the debris
Of daily life in a family
Where no one sees
The tracks of my lonely tears
The exhaustion

Humiliation
Consternation
Of living this way
It wasn't what I imagined
Not what I bargained for
Not that picture perfect
Martha Stewart
Road to domestic diligence
I dreamed about
Just last night.

At the top of the stairs
I turn the corner
Slaloming through the obstacle course
Dodging dirty clothes
Old newspapers and magazines
Towels, sheets
A laundry basket
Laying on its side
Solitary shoes
Of course, a few more socks
And finally a misplaced school bag
Misplaced?
Is anything misplaced
In such a mangled universe
Of random artifacts?
Maybe it's my distorted perception?
Perhaps everything is perfectly in place
And I am profoundly out of sorts.

Yes, out of sorts I am
Looking for love
Lonely, alone, tormented inside
I peer into my bedroom
Reminding myself
It has not been vandalized
It's only a weekday evening
There amid piles and piles
Of pillows and blankets
Are what keeps her covered
Far more distant from me
Than she ever realizes
Multiple years of hurt and pain
Addiction, co-dependence
Need lots of layering for protection
Against rejection, dejection
Tarnished dreams
Marriage held together
At the seams
The pain of infertility
Living in a sea
Of changing community
Subtle barriers of kids, parents
Work, email
Late night tiredness
Too many things to do
Intimacy moments
Far too few.

I stop and try to recall
What am I looking for after all
Not hungry for food
Lonely but no one is home
If I have to go it alone
Find me my paper and pen
Here is an old friend
I think I'll write a poem.

MY SISTER, MY BRIDE

On the occasion of 37 years of marriage

We were young and in love
As we prepared for that cosmic union
On a sunny southern afternoon
Way back when.

I knew you were my Sister, my Bride
The one for whom
My heart had opened wide
The passion of our love
The flame of our soul connection
Brought us to stand side-by-side
Under that beautifully-quilted *huppah*
Aspiring to unify the Holy Blessed One
And the Shechinah
In our married life together.
So we promised
So we aspired.

But did we have any clue of what challenges
Hardships, obstacles and pain was to greet us?
In between work and play
We laughed, made Shabbos
Created communities, shared with friends
Spent time on Lac des Sables and Lake Loudon
Even managed to spend a year

In the Holy City of Jerusalem
At the time of the first intifada.
But life unfolded with bumps and starts
Very quickly there were wrinkles
In the tapestry of our love
How did we survive
Conflicted late nights
Thursday night fights
Various infections
Pouty feelings of rejection
Abandonment fears
Rising up from early years
Love was not easy
Love was not kind.

Even as a we raised a young baby boy
The kitchen was chronically a mess
It seemed like an awful regress
To the same old shit
Over and over and over
I was tyrannical
You were the roommate from hell
Domestic life was certainly not swell
Things did not gel.
This was not what I imagined love to be.

Then hit the years of infertility
So much wait and see
Maybe
Maybe not

Simply told
We were courageous and bold
And chronically in pain
Willing to try again
Miscarriage of three
Why did this happen to me, to you
Who knew that this was part of love?
Then came number two
An energy dynamo appeared out of the blue
A fireball baby girl
Sent our life into a whirl
Four crammed in an apartment for three
While trying to work
Underemployment
Rabbinic deployment
The layers of pain
Again and again
So much more
So much more.

But we endured and persevered
Saw therapists and learned imago
Prayed and laughed
Always, always making Shabbos
Eventually landing in our
Forever home.

Blessings and complications
Creativity and other fascinations
Who knew if we would make it

But we persevered
Never gave up
Remembering the love
Remembering the original promise
With great difficulty we created a family
Even if family time was over-rated.
Child psychologists and ADHD meds
Occupational therapy and
Sensory integration diets
PTA trauma meetings
And some quiet moments of breathing
Remembering to love
Watching the children grow
Each in their own dawdling and bolting ways
Supporting each other
In our journeys in the world
Friendship truly deep
We managed to keep
The love alive
Even at times to thrive.

Who ever thought it would be this way?
I must say
As the children grew
High school, college
Therapeutic boarding school
Rehab and more
Books and CDs
Lecture and concerts
Congregations and university classes

Life persisted in the face of the absurdity of it all.
In moments the air would clear
And you were there, my dear
My companion and friend
My wife and lover in life
My Sister, my bride
The one for whom these arms opened wide.

Aging is happening
What was once young is maturing
Parents have died
Social security and medicare
Characterize our lives now
The children have their own lives
A glass artist, a chef
We have ours
And a cute dog named Yentl
There continues to be creativity
Laughter and love
Shabbos guests and nights of song
Just like we have been doing all along.
And you believed in me
You believed in us
You held onto to the dream
In the midst of the fog
In the midst of the mess.
And here we are
Thirty seven years and counting
Thank you for being my partner, my friend
Couldn't imagine any other life

Thanks for being you
Thanks for being my love, my wife
Thank you for being mother of our children
Thank you for being my business partner
At the Raphael Inn
Above all
Thanks for being the one in whom
My soul delights
Happy Anniversary.

SAND CASTLES DON'T LAST FOREVER

There they are
Playfully building a sand-castle
On the beach
My wife, my son, my daughter
A sand-castle
That will last
What? A few hours?
Only until high tide
Washes it all away.
Not much longer than that
Not fifteen years
Definitely not that long
Not even twelve years.

Soon my son will be a young man
Creating his own world
My daughter, one day
Will grow to be a woman
Busy with life and love
We probably won't
Build sand-castles any more
And my wife and I
May be just too old
To schlep our beach chairs
To the ocean.
So for these moments
Enjoy the building of

A castle in the sand
Imbibe the holiness of this special moment
Before all is washed away
Leaving only trace remnants
Of its eternal presence.

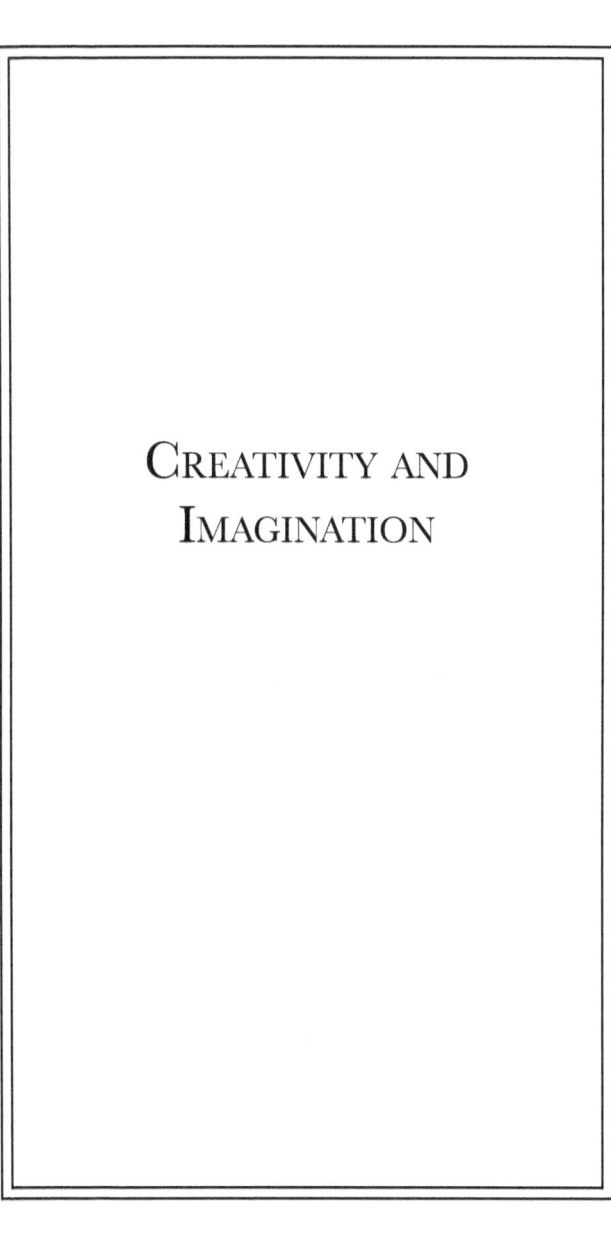

CREATIVITY AND
IMAGINATION

WIND

Wind howls wickedly and wildly
Feverishly dancing and randomly raging
At it traverses the terrain of the wide open plain
While trees shudder stoically
Shaken and awakened from serenity
As yet another squall of kinetic frenzy
Sweeps across the naked landscape
Hurling leaves, branches, brambles
And billows of dust
From mountain top to river bed
With unceasing certainty.

Like a song sung to an unsuspecting audience
The wind booms out its rhythmic melody
A cyclical chant of power and passion
A deep bass roar
Punctuated periodically
With momentary haunting silences
The dwindling pause of an in breath
Followed rapidly by gusting choruses
Yielding resonant reverberating encores.

And as the wind blows
I, a male mammal at mid-life
An embodied being with sensory receptors
Contemplate this panoramic scene before my eyes
Wondering with ever-present subjectivity

Am I ever really safe as I walk this planet?
Is anything safe in face of the turbulent
Unpredictability of Mother Nature?

And further, am I but an observer
A passive bystander
Seeing with my eyes
Hearing with my ears
Feeling sensation with a body layering of skin
As these atmospheric masses
Of wild and wanton wind
Sprint across and spiral around
This often quiet and quaint countryside
Nestled in this unknown and innocuous corner
Of this enigmatic entity we call Planet Earth?

Am I simply a spectator
A witnessing onlooker
An interplanetary explorer of strange new worlds
Passionately peering out
The window of my spacecraft
At this fragile, sometimes frail
Blue ball floating in deep space?

Or perhaps like the trees and bushes
The animals and fishes
The birds, bees, wildlife and wilderness
I, too, am part of this
Eternal merging, melding, meeting
Of earth and atmosphere, land and sky

A monadic I
Interwoven into the fabric of life
Yet so easily buffeted around
By the winds of time
The bellowing forces
Of gargantuan jet stream power
That may very well render me
Insignificant, inconsequential
But another speck of cosmic dust
Moving through eternity
To destinations unknown
Mercilessly subject to the gusts and lulls
Of shifting climatological and
Geological conditions
Created far beyond the immediacy
Of my very existence.

As the tempestuous winds continue to rage,
I wonder
Am I ever really safe as I walk this planet?
How can I make my way amid
The sound and fury of life
Holding fast to the earth beneath my feet
As the winds of personal and cultural change
Howl incessantly?

As essence dust is stirred up deep within my being
I notice my soul waves untethered in the wind.
What is really going on here?
Is it the echoes of existential angst

An awareness of human limitation
Knowing the inevitability
Of death and powerlessness
In the face of nature's fury?

Or is it urban despair
A city boy in the country
Painfully aware of my awkward otherness
And disparate disconnection from Mother Nature
On a wonderfully windy day?

Or perhaps it's really the dilemma of a poet
Seeing the patterns of cosmic perfection
In the daily weather
Watching, wondering, writing
Waiting for a poem to emerge,
Then writing some more?

Maybe, just maybe
I should put down my pen and paper
Put on a warm coat
And go outside for a walk in the woods
Hang out in the wilderness of my soul
Instead of pondering the passion of the wind
While sitting indoors and looking out the window.

Pens and Poetry

Pens and poetry are passions of mine
Each in their own ways
Reminding me to remember
To re-embody
To know inwardly and with depth
The essence and essential nectar of life.

Pens print on paper
Ephemeral expressions of eternity
Etching in manifest form
Remnants and elements
Stories and tales
Awakenings and encounters
Loves and passions
Of the ever-evolving
Human spirit.

And poetry
Words castles of the mind
Reveal ever-changing tales
Of the human heart
Poignant pristine perspectives
Multi-fold expressions
Of God's creation
As revealed in various vicissitudes
Of the drama of life.

And this poem
Written with pen and ink
Upon crisp, consecrated paper
Is an outpouring
Of spirit, mind and body
A delightful delineation
Depicting a brief moment of time
A passing thought, an image
A sacred impression of mind
Birthed into life through the feed canal
Of a fountain pen
Flowing forth from wet womb of the ink reservoir
As if from the source of existence itself.

Like an ancient scribal artist
Carving wisdom into
Precambrian rock formations
I write these words of poetry
Crafting a serendipitous meeting
Of the mundane and the divine
Gracefully fusing pen, ink, and paper
Watching meticulously and methodically
As moist ink scribed upon this page
Dries ever-so-slowly
Leaving behind an indelible, delicate imprint
Of God matter
Etched forever in the data bank of soul
In this moment
Here-Now
And for eternity.*

* Published in *Pennant–A Publication of the Pen Collectors of America*,
  (Spring-Summer 2004)

Thoughts on the Super Bowl

Gladiators of the twenty-first century
Olympians of skill, strength and prowess
Agile in athletic acumen
Valiantly jousting invading adversaries
Carrying the golden sphere
Through arches of triumph
While god-intoxicated cheering armies
Watch voluptuous, naval-bejeweled maidens
Vestal virgins of victory
Dance sacred sensual rites
Adulating hallowed heroes of the Holy Grail.

SITTING IN STARBUCKS

Cars and vans, trucks and busses whiz by
While white-haired, well-dressed ladies
Stop and chat
And rare and perfectly placed trees
Quiver in the wind
Dancing to the constant hubbub
Of urban pulsations
All seen from the other side
Of this storefront window
A clear panoramic lens of vision
To the outside world of resplendent vitality
While inside another exquisite dimension unfolds
Subtle soft jazz pleasantly permeates the space
Replete with cushy comfortable chairs
Tiled tables and carpeted floors
The aromatic scent of coffee
Wafts through the air
Penetrated intermittently
With the whirring sounds of a bean grinder
As the cash register registers
Yet another purchase of Starbucks Coffee
The exotic, auburn elixir of life
A frequently called upon solution
To the demands of post-millennial stress
Espresso, latte, cappuccino, decaf, mocha
And more
So satisfyingly fulfilling primal yearnings

Of my caffeine-starved body
In the gentle pause of this transcendent moment
I am renewed, re-animated with soul juice
This is the pause that refreshes
Good to the last drop
Yet even with soul thirst quenched
An inexplicable impulse of uncertainty emerges
From deep within
Suddenly I lose my bearings
Feel untethered in the galaxy
And with deep cosmic curiosity
I wonder to myself in earth shattering silence
Am I sitting in this Starbucks
Or at the one down the street?

Tasty Hamantaschen

The wonder of wild worldly women
Wantonly and willfully emerging at Purim
Like freshly-baked sweet hamantaschen
Hot and steamy inside
Succulent, sensuous, lustful and lascivious
Tender and tasty to the touch of the tongue.
From whence do they emerge?
To where do they return?
As a tipsy Queen Esther slips off in the night
The wanton wild woman
Withdraws and wilts back
To a pensive, passive and parve predicament
Somewhat frosty, flaky and dry on the outside
A bit nutty inside
With small broken corners crumbling apart.
This is the Mystery of Purim!
Ah, how I love to eat fresh hamantaschen
On Purim night!

Morning Is Like an Old Lover

Morning is like an old lover
Vaguely familiar
Seductively beckoning me into relationship
And me—I'm not coy, just ambivalent
Reluctant to respond
Preferring to remain disengaged
Under the covers
Fantasizing about self-pleasuring
Not yet ready for encounter
With the myriad of complexities
Intimacies, demands and needs
That fill a day.

So for a little longer
I linger in the twilight
Of morning fog
Knowing that sooner or later
I will relent
And be seduced
Back into familiar pathways
Of love, lust, and passion
The particularities that make up a day.

Ah morning
Old lover that you are
Even if I've not yet
Brushed my teeth

I guess I can greet you
With open eyes
A gentle kiss
A stretch and a sigh
Responding to the lure
Of morning foreplay
Causing me to awaken and rise.
I guess I'll take off all my clothes
Will you accompany me into the shower?
I have always loved to do that with you
To be massaged and awakened
In my nakedness
Invited into love, life, and another day
By warm, soothing streams of water.
Ah yes, how sweet it is
To meet, greet and merge
With an old lover
Makes the day
A bit sweeter.

BECAUSE

Because the late hours of the night
       leave the stomach hungry and growling;
       and

because a stressful life catalyzes
       a thirst for alcohol
       to numb the intensity and stimulation;
       and

because loneliness induces longing and lust
       for companionship and sex;
       and

because friends like to gather together
       over food and drink;
       and

because good music eases a weary soul;
       and

because it's warm inside
       on a chilly fall night;

because of all these reasons,
       and probably many more
       a crowd of people are wining and dining
       shmoozing and cruising

at this trendy local jazz bar
with funky music
reverberating in the air;
and

because I don't feel like talking to anyone
I am sitting here alone
scribbling these words on paper
in between bites of eggplant parmigiana
and sips of white zinfandel wine

because I want to write a poem that
begins and ends with
because.

Autumn Snow

Wordless moments unfold
As I sit in awe
Watching a wild and wily winter wonderland
Majestically revealed before my eyes
Temporarily and tentatively interrupting
The meandering mind-stream of meditative
Thoughts, perceptions, fantasies
And twice-told tales of
A future that isn't yet
And a past long gone.

When with a gentle in breathe
And conscious out breathe
I invite my eyes
To focus on the graceful falling of
Unanticipated October snow
The flotsam and jetsam
Of many myriad mind forms of
Meaningless moments of
Mental masturbation
Stop suddenly and swiftly
Allowing me to notice
The gentle beauty of nature
In its erratic, exotic exhibition
Of extreme autumn weather.

In the graced mystery of this
Magical meteorological moment
With instinctive certainty I know that
I am but a snowflake in the passing of time
A single, solitary soul
Interwoven into the woof and warp
Of the very fabric of creation itself.

But nonetheless
Even dressed with hat, scarf and gloves
Boots and a warm coat
It is bloody cold outside for October.

A Post-9/11 Elegy

Written on an Amtrak to Manhattan, NY

Off in the distance
I see the world-famous
Manhattan skyline
Like digits of a hand
Reaching to the sky.
Through the haze of the maze
I notice how
The largest fingers
Have been amputated
Cut to the ground
Zero
Disappeared
Like a magician's
Sleight of the hand illusion.
All in the name of
Religious fervor.
What a strange surgical procedure.

UNDER A FRAGILE THATCHED ROOF

Under a fragile thatched roof
Full-breasted mother moon
And a subtle glitter band
Of twinkling stars
Transparently peek through
From the heavenly spheres
To this temporary
Transient human realm
Naked, undefended against the elements
I sit in silent contemplation
In this sukkah of peace
Unprotected and vulnerable
In the face of life's ever-changing transitions
Knowing one turn of the cosmic clock
One subtle stopped heartbeat
An unanticipated wind of change
Death, divorce, destruction
Hurricane, shadow eruptions of hell
Fire, flood, fatality or fanaticism
Or any one of a million other maybes
Can wipe away this moment
This life
This most fragile sukkah
This life story I call my own
And bring in its wake
Who knows what
Where

Why
Or why not.
And all I can do
Is live with the unfolding
Of the blessing and the curse
And choose life
As well as I am able to.

So in this temporary
Sukkah of peace
I am reminded
To harvest in holy humility
A sacred sense
Of how good it is
To be alive
How good it is
For sisters and brothers
To sit, sing and pray
Together as one.

SELF-DISCOVERY: A THREE-PART JOURNEY

Part I: Being Lost

Staring in the mirror on New Year's Day
Who is this person I see?
A balding, middle-aged man
Overweight, sad and lonely
Shoulders hunched, body ballooning out of shape
The once ever-present glorious gleam in my eyes
Now, at least temporarily tarnished by tension
Fears of failure and fading fortunes
Shadowy shades of struggle and shame
Reverberating and resonating in my being
In complex cascading waves of anxiety
Quite clearly the result of
Trials and tribulations of times of economic woe
Planetary warfare, melting polar caps
Poisoned water, chemical toxicity
Unending attacks of email, Facebook
Uninvited internet intrusions
And so much more, so so much more
Consuming time and mind
Leaving in its wake
Saturated, diminished, and depleted soul vitality
Irritation, impatience, exhaustion
Intermittent boredom, iconoclastic ennui
And a pounding pulsating proliferation of
Unending existential angst.

Who is this man I see
Reflected in the mirror today
At this exact, emergent moment of time?
Have I been absent for so long
That I hardly recognize myself anymore?
Whatever happened to that zestful, playful
Creative, charismatic, compassionate
Inspired, inventive, intuitive, and insightful guy
I once knew, way back whenever that was?
Have the ravages of manifold moments
Of midlife melancholia
(Welbutrin and Prozac not withstanding)
Plus career callings, cranky kids
A post-menopausal wife
Plumbers, electricians, a leaky roof
Leaky faucets needing fixing
And too many late night fixings
Of chocolate or cheese
Plus sensory sessions of solitary self-pleasuring
And plenty of other predictable
Habitual, crazy and compulsive
Moments of self-soothing and
Surrender to subterranean urges and purges
Taken their terrifying toll
Leaving me exactly as I am
In this immediate moment
Whether I am present or not?
Whether I like it or not?

It seems to me that somehow or other
I am left wildly wondering
If what I am seeing is really what I am seeing
Or merely a vague, ruminating reflection
A distorted perception of who I think I am
When I am not really thinking at all?
Am I actually seeing myself
As I truly have become
Or only glimpsing fragmentary feeling figments
Of my most limited and limiting judgmental
mind
A shadow of what really is
Reflected on the wall of the cavernous cave
I have created in my exceptionally ephemeral
Extraneous transitory transitional mind?

This is the dilemma I encounter
Standing in front of the mirror
On this New Year's Day.

Part II: Returning Home

Continuing to stare
At the silhouetted reflection in the mirror
Taking a deep breathe of annual renewal
With a subtle gift of grace
Meditative mind emerges
Out of the morass of the mundane
Guided gently I gaze inwardly
Observing but not allowing

The endless aura of existential angst
Nor savory succulent waves of self-pity
To invade and pervade the atmosphere.

Breathing in, breathing out
Breathing in, breathing out
Internal vision is awakened, activated
Awareness shifts from foreground to background
Moving from cluttered contents of psyche
To the conscious witness of what is.
Once again seeing with lucidity and sanity
A concise and composed clarity re-emerges
As if for the first time.
Having been gracefully graced
Instantaneously, I return home
From the far away shores
Of reckless rampant rumination
Seeing beyond disguised distorted
Fleeting perceptions
Of fickle flickering fires on the walls of the cave.
From deep within this clarity of consciousness
Flashing before my eyes
I see the patterned soul prints
Of so many lifetimes
Having lived and died
Having loved and lost.
The soul having played out
The drama of life for G!d.
Through the eye of contemplation,
I re-cognize myself

Awakening from a somnambulant sleep
Knowing as I have always known
That this precise, pristine
Exact moment of my life journey
Is but a fragmentary fleeting fraction
Of infinite time and history
That this story I call my life
Today, on this New Year's Day
At this mediocre midlife juncture
Is but a speck
Or perhaps just a fleck
In the vast expanse
Of eternal eons and ages
Never-ending cycles
Endless endings and beginnings.
Lifetimes lived, death times died
Life stories told, retold
Destiny yet to unfold.
All of this in this moment
In this now.

As I witness this unfolding vision before my eyes
I know with absolute certainty
That nothing whatsoever is absolutely certain
That the challenges of this day
The story fragments of this man
Whose image is momentarily made manifest
In the mirror on the morning of New Year's Day
Reveal and conceal
A blatant and boldly apparent

Invisible opportunity for awakening
Arousing a subtle, tender budding
Of consciousness
That potently and potentially can yield
A knowing of self, time, G!d, and universe
In brazenly bold new ways
Birthing and rebirthing soul and psyche
Healing and making whole being and body
Now
In this moment
In this time
In this year.

Part III: Now What?

Deepening contemplative concentration
On this New Year's morning
I can now behold
The manifest multiplicity of all that is
Seeing both the drama trauma
Of this midlife melodrama
And the vast spectrum of cosmic time
The panoramic soul story
Unfolding before my very eyes
Scintillating radiantly and dancing a pas-de-deux
In this magical magnificent mirror.

In-breath, out-breath
And I wonder: now what?
It is true:

I am over-weight, broke and in a funk
It is True:
The me that I think I am
Is at one and the same time
Also a transmigrating soul in evolution
Eternal spirit housed in a finite and aging body.
This is true, and that is True!
All that is, isn't always as it appears.
And what appears is at one and the same time
More and less than what is
Depending upon the vantage point of perception
This is simply the way that it is.
Bidden or not, God is present
And that is the Truth.

Now what? I wonder.
Then it all comes back to me
Resolving resolutely
With a New Year's resolution:
Meditate more!
Eat less cookies and chocolate!
Appreciate the infinite cycles
Of death, rebirth and renewal!
Stay awake to the enigmatic wonder and mystery
Of evolving spirit embodied in matter!
And by all means: spend less time on Facebook
And much more time seeing God face-to-face.
Much more time seeing God face-to-face.
Welcome home! Have a Happy New Year!
Have a Happy Renew Year!

JUVENILIA

Who Am I?

my mind turns
my cigarette smolders
like an ash falling out of place
i utter my thoughts, trivialities

my opinions are expressed
on bathroom walls
they are washed off
forever gone to waste

who am i?
when will i depart?
does it matter?
who gives a damn?

life is interminable
like a beach
but i'm a grain of sand
being washed out to sea

and when my cigarette is dead
so am i
but my package isn't buried with me
it lives on and on.

SILENCE

noise
no noise:
      silence

people
no people:
      silence

no bomb
bomb:
      silence

On the Formation of a
Joint Committee

*Written 59 years before legalization of
cannabis in Canada*

The House of Commons
And all their Lawmens
Issued a petition
Forming a Royal Commission
To offer educated views
On drugs and their abuse
These men shall research and really try
To see where the legalization problem does lie.
The men in Ottawa accept suggestion
Pertinent, of course, to a pertinent question
So I went there
And spoke with Mr. Pierre
Mr. P.M., I politely stated
I hope my opinions won't be under-rated
I think this commission is actually a joke
Unless these men are willing to smoke
What you need of course, it seems to me
Is the formation of a Joint Committee
Then and only then
Can these educated men
Release their frustrations
Through hallucinations.
Ridiculous, ridiculous! the P.M. cried

So I left the capital and merely sighed.
Three days later I received by post
A letter from Parliament's host
Dear Mr. Raphael, the letter said,
I considered your suggestion
Last night while in bed
Personally, I sincerely hope
One day we can all legally do dope
But now, in this present day
The letter went on to say
We can't make dope legal for any head
Until Conservative John quietly drops dead
Yours very truly, the letter came to an end
Signed Pierre, your very good friend.
Well, then I went to see 'Ol Dief
I was greeted amiably by the former chief
I said, Listen John, what do you say
If all marijuana laws were thrown away?
Well, as I see it, he began to rap
And piled on a bunch of crap
About how it's bad and kills
And it's worse than taking pills
And it leads to harder stuff
Then to crime, then gruff.
Figuring it was hopeless, I left it at that
And went to the closet to get my hat
Stay for some food, he said to me
So I remained and Mrs. Dief served tea
While casually talking politics, like the NDP
I reached into my pocket, and felt a tablet of LSD

Slyly I waited for Dief to look up
Then dropped the tab into his cup
I don't remember what else I said
But five minutes later John went out of his head
First he ran up and down the house
Then started crying, saying he saw a mouse.
Legalize dope! Legalize dope! He began to say
We can't wait another day.
Then he began to yell and scream
But then I awoke and realized it was all a dream.
Well anyway, soon
The Royal Commission report will come out
No matter what it says, Dief will shout
P.M. Trudeau will just sit there
Wondering why he's losing his hair.
Personally, I think nothing will be done
But I guess it's still fun
To remember that dream which I had
So I guess politicians can't be all bad.
In the meantime, all I can do is hope
Maybe one day, we'll be smoking dope.

The Da'at Institute
Melrose Park, PA, 19027
drsimcha@daatinstitute.net
daatinstitute.net

The DA'AT INSTITUTE is dedicated to providing death awareness education and professional development training. Working in consultation with synagogues, churches, hospice programs and other types of community organizations, the DA'AT INSTITUTE offers:

1. *Educational Programs* on death, dying, bereavement, and the spirituality of end-of-life issues and concerns.

2. *Professional Development Training* to clergy, health care and mental health professionals and educators working with the dying and bereaved.

3. *Bereavement and Hospice Counseling Services* to individuals and families through counseling, professional referral and bereavement support groups.

4. *Rituals of Transition* for dying, burial, bereavement, unveiling and memorialization, helping families create meaningful rituals of passage.

5. *Printed and Audio-Visual Resources* on the various facets of dealing with grief and loss, and on the spirituality of death and afterlife.

Originally from Montreal, Canada, Simcha Paull Raphael, Ph.D. is Founding Director of the DA'AT Institute for Death Awareness, Advocacy and Training. He received a Master of Arts in History and Philosophy of Religion from Concordia University, a doctorate in Psychology from the California Institute of Integral Studies and was ordained as a Pastoral Rabbi by Reb Zalman Schachter-Shalomi. He has served as Adjunct Professor at LaSalle University, Temple University and in the Aleph Ordination Program. Currently, he works as a psychotherapist and spiritual director in the Philadelphia area, and is on Faculty of the Art of Dying Institute of One Spirit Learning Alliance. He has published six book on death and Judaism including the groundbreaking book *Jewish Views of the Afterlife* and a collection of poetry, *Echoes from the Ashes: Holocaust Poems of Life, Death and Re-Birth*. Reb Simcha and his wife, Rabbi Geela Rayzel Raphael live in the Philadelphia area with their son Yigdal and daughter Hallel.